jB
C61608

RL 7.6 PV 1.0

CY

PRESIDENTS

BILL CLINTON

A MyReportLinks.com Book

Tim O'Shei

MyReportLinks.com Books

an imprint of

Enslow Publishers, Inc.

Box 398, 40 Industrial Road
Berkeley Heights, NJ 07922
USA

MyReportLinks.com Books, an imprint of Enslow Publishers, Inc. MyReportLinks is a trademark of Enslow Publishers, Inc.

Library of Congress Cataloging-in-Publication Data

O'Shei, Tim.
  Bill Clinton / Tim O'Shei.
    p. cm. – (Presidents)
Summary: A biography of the forty-second president of the United States, who was only the second president to be impeached. Includes Internet links to Web sites, source documents, and photographs related to Bill Clinton.
Includes bibliographical references and index.
  ISBN 0-7660-5149-8
  1. Clinton, Bill, 1946–Juvenile literature. 2. Presidents–United States–Biography–Juvenile literature. [1. Clinton, Bill, 1946– 2. Presidents.] I. Title. II. Series.
  E886.O83 2003
  973.929'092–dc22

2003011657

Printed in the United States of America

10 9 8 7 6 5 4 3 2 1

To Our Readers:
Through the purchase of this book, you and your library gain access to the Report Links that specifically back up this book.
The Publisher will provide access to the Report Links that back up this book and will keep these Report Links up to date on **www.myreportlinks.com** for three years from the book's first publication date.
We have done our best to make sure all Internet addresses in this book were active and appropriate when we went to press. However, the author and the Publisher have no control over, and assume no liability for, the material available on those Internet sites or on other Web sites they may link to.
The usage of the MyReportLinks.com Books Web site is subject to the terms and conditions stated on the Usage Policy Statement on **www.myreportlinks.com**.
A password may be required to access the Report Links that back up this book. The password is found on the bottom of page 4 of this book.
Any comments or suggestions can be sent by e-mail to comments@myreportlinks.com or to the address on the back cover.

Photo Credits: AP/Wide World Photos, pp. 11, 19, 26, 32, 34, 39; Cable News Network, pp. 24, 44; Clinton Presidential Center, pp. 13, 22; © Corel Corporation, pp. 1 (background), 3; © 2003 Time, Inc., pp. 40, 42; Georgetown University, p. 20; Library of Congress, pp. 27, 36; Michael Schuman Photo, p. 14; MyReportLinks.com Books, p. 4; Courtesy of the White House, pp. 1, 29, 31; University of Arkansas at Little Rock and the Hempstead County Economic Development Corporation, p. 16;

Cover Photo: Courtesy of the White House

Contents

MyReportLinks.com Books
Great Books, Great Links, Great for Research!

MyReportLinks.com Books present the information you need to learn about your report subject. In addition, they show you where to go on the Internet for more information. The pre-evaluated Report Links that back up this book are kept up to date on **www.myreportlinks.com**. With the purchase of a MyReportLinks.com Books title, you and your library gain access to the Report Links that specifically back up that book. The Report Links save hours of research time and link to dozens—even hundreds—of Web sites, source documents, and photos related to your report topic.

Please see "To Our Readers" on the Copyright page for important information about this book, the MyReportLinks.com Books Web site, and the Report Links that back up this book.

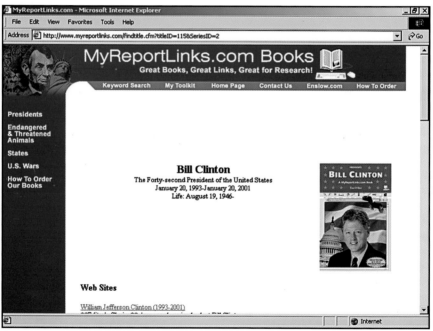

Access:

The Publisher will provide access to the Report Links that back up this book and will try to keep these Report Links up to date on our Web site for three years from the book's first publication date. Please enter **PBC6428** if asked for a password.

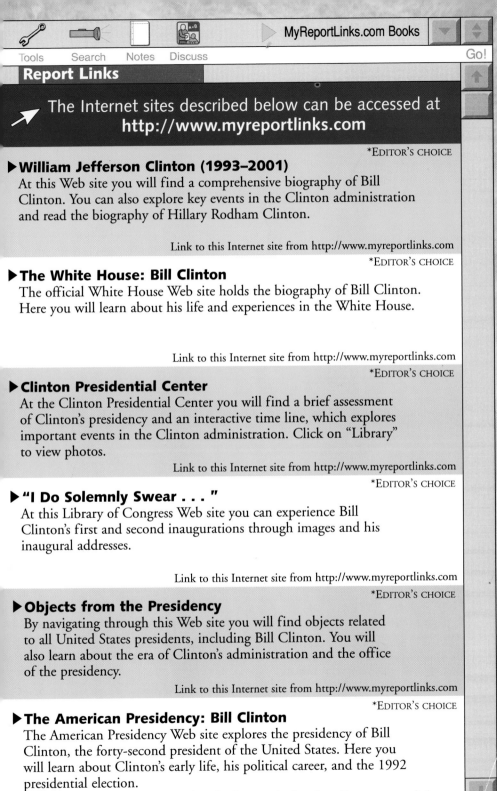
The Internet sites described below can be accessed at
http://www.myreportlinks.com

*EDITOR'S CHOICE

▶ **William Jefferson Clinton (1993–2001)**
At this Web site you will find a comprehensive biography of Bill
Clinton. You can also explore key events in the Clinton administration
and read the biography of Hillary Rodham Clinton.

Link to this Internet site from http://www.myreportlinks.com

*EDITOR'S CHOICE

▶ **The White House: Bill Clinton**
The official White House Web site holds the biography of Bill Clinton.
Here you will learn about his life and experiences in the White House.

Link to this Internet site from http://www.myreportlinks.com

*EDITOR'S CHOICE

▶ **Clinton Presidential Center**
At the Clinton Presidential Center you will find a brief assessment
of Clinton's presidency and an interactive time line, which explores
important events in the Clinton administration. Click on "Library"
to view photos.

Link to this Internet site from http://www.myreportlinks.com

*EDITOR'S CHOICE

▶ **"I Do Solemnly Swear . . . "**
At this Library of Congress Web site you can experience Bill
Clinton's first and second inaugurations through images and his
inaugural addresses.

Link to this Internet site from http://www.myreportlinks.com

*EDITOR'S CHOICE

▶ **Objects from the Presidency**
By navigating through this Web site you will find objects related
to all United States presidents, including Bill Clinton. You will
also learn about the era of Clinton's administration and the office
of the presidency.

Link to this Internet site from http://www.myreportlinks.com

*EDITOR'S CHOICE

▶ **The American Presidency: Bill Clinton**
The American Presidency Web site explores the presidency of Bill
Clinton, the forty-second president of the United States. Here you
will learn about Clinton's early life, his political career, and the 1992
presidential election.

Link to this Internet site from http://www.myreportlinks.com

Report Links

The Internet sites described below can be accessed at
http://www.myreportlinks.com

▶**About Jim Brady**
During his first term in office, Bill Clinton signed a gun-control law named
after former Press Secretary James Brady. You can read a brief biography of
Brady at this site.

Link to this Internet site from http://www.myreportlinks.com

▶**The American Presidency: Al Gore, Jr.**
The American Presidency Web site provides a brief biography of Al Gore.
Here you will learn about his political career, vice presidency, and 2000
campaign for presidency.

Link to this Internet site from http://www.myreportlinks.com

▶**American Presidents: Bill Clinton**
The American President Web site provides essential "Life Facts" and "Did you
know?" trivia about Bill Clinton. You can also read a letter written by Bill
Clinton about why he did not want to participate in the Vietnam War.

Link to this Internet site from http://www.myreportlinks.com

▶**Chelsea Clinton leaves the nest**
This CNN article discusses Chelsea Clinton's first day at Stanford University.
Here you can read about some of the special accommodations made for her at
the university and view pictures of Chelsea with her parents.

Link to this Internet site from http://www.myreportlinks.com

▶**The Clinton Years**
PBS's *Frontline* takes an in-depth look at the Clinton administration. Here
you can read interviews that look back on the early days of Clinton's campaign
for president, his transition into the presidency, and the turmoil and success
he encountered along the way.

Link to this Internet site from http://www.myreportlinks.com

▶**Clinton's Legacy**
On this site from *U.S. News & World Report*, you can learn about the
presidency of Bill Clinton. View a photo album, and read articles related
to major events during his two terms in office.

Link to this Internet site from http://www.myreportlinks.com

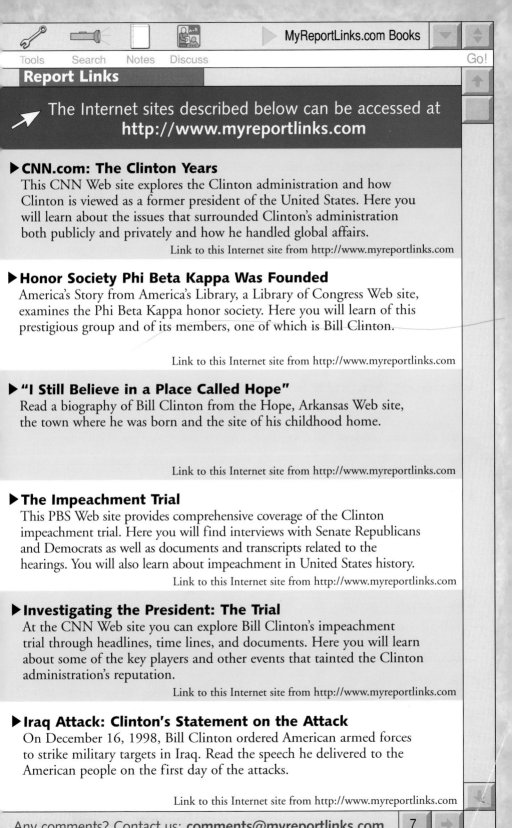

The Internet sites described below can be accessed at
http://www.myreportlinks.com

▶ **CNN.com: The Clinton Years**
This CNN Web site explores the Clinton administration and how
Clinton is viewed as a former president of the United States. Here you
will learn about the issues that surrounded Clinton's administration
both publicly and privately and how he handled global affairs.

Link to this Internet site from http://www.myreportlinks.com

▶ **Honor Society Phi Beta Kappa Was Founded**
America's Story from America's Library, a Library of Congress Web site,
examines the Phi Beta Kappa honor society. Here you will learn of this
prestigious group and of its members, one of which is Bill Clinton.

Link to this Internet site from http://www.myreportlinks.com

▶ **"I Still Believe in a Place Called Hope"**
Read a biography of Bill Clinton from the Hope, Arkansas Web site,
the town where he was born and the site of his childhood home.

Link to this Internet site from http://www.myreportlinks.com

▶ **The Impeachment Trial**
This PBS Web site provides comprehensive coverage of the Clinton
impeachment trial. Here you will find interviews with Senate Republicans
and Democrats as well as documents and transcripts related to the
hearings. You will also learn about impeachment in United States history.

Link to this Internet site from http://www.myreportlinks.com

▶ **Investigating the President: The Trial**
At the CNN Web site you can explore Bill Clinton's impeachment
trial through headlines, time lines, and documents. Here you will learn
about some of the key players and other events that tainted the Clinton
administration's reputation.

Link to this Internet site from http://www.myreportlinks.com

▶ **Iraq Attack: Clinton's Statement on the Attack**
On December 16, 1998, Bill Clinton ordered American armed forces
to strike military targets in Iraq. Read the speech he delivered to the
American people on the first day of the attacks.

Link to this Internet site from http://www.myreportlinks.com

Back	Forward	Stop	Review	Home	Explore	Favorites	History

Report Links

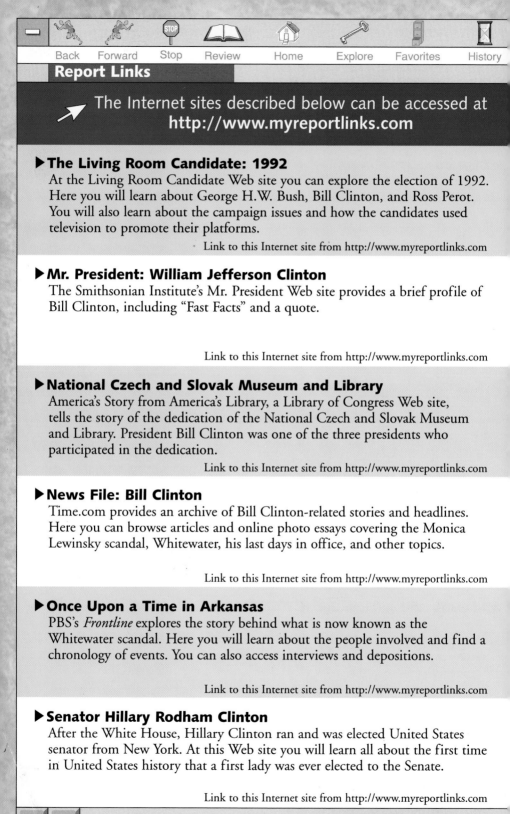

➤ The Internet sites described below can be accessed at
http://www.myreportlinks.com

▶ The Living Room Candidate: 1992

At the Living Room Candidate Web site you can explore the election of 1992.
Here you will learn about George H.W. Bush, Bill Clinton, and Ross Perot.
You will also learn about the campaign issues and how the candidates used
television to promote their platforms.

Link to this Internet site from http://www.myreportlinks.com

▶ Mr. President: William Jefferson Clinton

The Smithsonian Institute's Mr. President Web site provides a brief profile of
Bill Clinton, including "Fast Facts" and a quote.

Link to this Internet site from http://www.myreportlinks.com

▶ National Czech and Slovak Museum and Library

America's Story from America's Library, a Library of Congress Web site,
tells the story of the dedication of the National Czech and Slovak Museum
and Library. President Bill Clinton was one of the three presidents who
participated in the dedication.

Link to this Internet site from http://www.myreportlinks.com

▶ News File: Bill Clinton

Time.com provides an archive of Bill Clinton-related stories and headlines.
Here you can browse articles and online photo essays covering the Monica
Lewinsky scandal, Whitewater, his last days in office, and other topics.

Link to this Internet site from http://www.myreportlinks.com

▶ Once Upon a Time in Arkansas

PBS's *Frontline* explores the story behind what is now known as the
Whitewater scandal. Here you will learn about the people involved and find a
chronology of events. You can also access interviews and depositions.

Link to this Internet site from http://www.myreportlinks.com

▶ Senator Hillary Rodham Clinton

After the White House, Hillary Clinton ran and was elected United States
senator from New York. At this Web site you will learn all about the first time
in United States history that a first lady was ever elected to the Senate.

Link to this Internet site from http://www.myreportlinks.com

Report Links

The Internet sites described below can be accessed at
http://www.myreportlinks.com

▶ *Time for Kids Online:* **Bill Clinton's Moment Of Truth**
At the *Time for Kids Online* Web site you can read a news article that
addresses the question of whether Clinton lied under oath.

Link to this Internet site from http://www.myreportlinks.com

▶ **War In Europe**
PBS's *Frontline* offers an in-depth look at the war in Kosovo and Serbia.
Here you can read interviews with the key players involved and learn
how the war was fought. You will also find facts and figures and a
chronology of events.

Link to this Internet site from http://www.myreportlinks.com

▶ **The White House: Hillary Rodham Clinton**
The official White House Web site holds the biography of Hillary
Rodham Clinton. Here you will learn about her life before becoming
first lady, her experiences in the White House, and her political career
after the White House.

Link to this Internet site from http://www.myreportlinks.com

▶ **The White House Historical Association**
Explore the rich history of the White House and the presidents of the
United States. You can also take a virtual tour of the White House, visit
the president's park, and experience past presidential inaugurations.

Link to this Internet site from http://www.myreportlinks.com

▶ **William Jefferson Clinton**
The Presidents of the United States Web site offers facts and figures on
Bill Clinton. Here you will find election results, a list of cabinet
members, historical documents, and media resources.

Link to this Internet site from http://www.myreportlinks.com

▶ *World Almanac for Kids Online:* **William
Jefferson Clinton**
World Almanac for Kids Online provides a useful introduction
to Bill Clinton and his administration.

Link to this Internet site from http://www.myreportlinks.com

1946—*May 17:* William J. Blythe II is killed in an automobile mishap three months before the birth of his son.

—*Aug. 19:* William J. Blythe III is born in Hope, Arkansas. He later becomes known as William J. Clinton.

1963—Meets President Kennedy on a trip to Washington, D.C.

1964—Begins freshman year at Georgetown University in Washington.

1968—Graduates from Georgetown; wins a Rhodes Scholarship and attends Oxford University in England.

1971—Leaves Oxford and enrolls in Yale Law School.

1973—Graduates from Yale; accepts a teaching position at the University of Arkansas.

1974—Unsuccessfully runs for Congress in Arkansas.

1975—*Oct. 11:* Marries Hillary Rodham.

1976—Elected attorney general of Arkansas.

1978—Elected governor of Arkansas.

1980—*Feb. 27:* Daughter Chelsea is born.

—Loses reelection bid for governor.

1982—Reelected governor.

1984—Reelected governor.

1986—Reelected governor to a four-year term.

1990—Reelected governor.

1992—Elected the forty-second president.

1993—Signs Brady Bill for gun control; North American Free Trade Agreement is approved.

1994—Independent counsel investigates the Whitewater affair.

1996—Signs welfare reform bill; is reelected president.

1998—Clinton's relationship with a White House intern is exposed.

—*Dec. 19:* Clinton is impeached by the House of Representatives.

1999—*Jan. 7:* Impeachment trial begins in the Senate.

—*Feb. 12:* Clinton is acquitted.

2000—Hillary Clinton becomes a senator from New York.

2001—*Jan.:* Bill Clinton leaves office.

Chapter 1

Hope For America, July 16, 1992

Bill Clinton stepped to the podium and let his eyes brush across the mass of people that filled every seat and aisle of Madison Square Garden. Every one of them was cheering, and they were doing it for him. With the speech he was about to give, the governor of Arkansas was accepting his political party's nomination for president of the United States.

His opponent was the current president, George Herbert Walker Bush. The Republican had led the United States through a successful war in the Middle East, but now the economy was faltering. People were losing jobs. Their investments were not paying off. They wanted a change. On the night of July 16, 1992, Clinton was going to tell both the crowd at the Democratic National Convention and the millions of people watching on national television that he could do better.

Bill Clinton, then governor of ▶ Arkansas, arrives in New York with his wife, Hillary, and his daughter, Chelsea, on July 12, 1992, to speak at the Democratic National Convention later that week.

▷ Motherly Love

The governor's mother had represented Arkansas as delegates from each of the fifty states cast their ballots for Clinton. "Madame Secretary" Virginia Clinton Kelley called out to the woman tallying the votes, "Arkansas proudly casts our forty-eight votes for our favorite son—and my son—Bill Clinton!"[1]

Now, as Clinton described his ideas for creating a better America, he thanked his mother for teaching him how to be tough. She had raised him with little money but a lot of love, and he was paying her back.

"You want to know where I get my fighting spirit?" Clinton said. "It all started with my mother." Then, pointing directly to his mom, he added, "Thank you, Mother. I love you."[2]

Clinton went on to describe how his grandfather had taught him about equality simply by the way he ran his grocery store. Clinton thanked his wife, Hillary, for teaching him about the value of helping children in need.

It was time, Clinton said, for President Bush to go. Washington needed new ideas, a new life, and he was ready to deliver. "We have to go beyond the brain-dead politics in Washington and give our people the kind of government they deserve," he said. "A government that works."[3]

▷ A Place Called Hope

Fifty-three minutes after he began talking, Clinton took his final breath, ready to deliver one last line. In just moments, he was to be joined on stage by his vice presidential running mate, Senator Al Gore, and their wives and children. Balloons would drop, and the music of Fleetwood Mac's song "Don't Stop" would boom through the speakers.

Tools   Search   Notes   Discuss   Go!

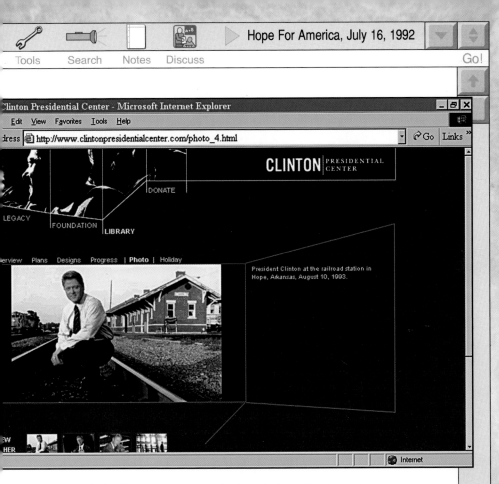

Clinton Presidential Center - Microsoft Internet Explorer

Edit   View   Favorites   Tools   Help

dress   http://www.clintonpresidentialcenter.com/photo_4.html   Go   Links

CLINTON | PRESIDENTIAL CENTER

DONATE

LEGACY   FOUNDATION   LIBRARY

erview   Plans   Designs   Progress | **Photo** | Holiday

President Clinton at the railroad station in Hope, Arkansas, August 10, 1993.

Internet

▲ *President Clinton poses in front of the train station in his hometown of Hope, Arkansas, in August 1993.*

That was all about to happen, but first, Clinton had to pay tribute to the small Arkansas town where he was born. His father had been killed three months before Bill was born, and Bill did not have a good relationship with his stepfather. His mother and grandparents had raised Bill Clinton to persevere through all those challenges.

Now, standing at this podium in New York City, Bill Clinton had clearly come far. He was only one step away from becoming president of the United States.

"I will end tonight where it all began for me," Clinton said, delivering a line suggested to him by his wife, Hillary. "I still believe in a place called Hope."[4]

Chapter 2 ▶

Small Town Boy, Big Dreams, 1946–1964

On the evening of May 17, 1946, a man named William Blythe was driving from Chicago, Illinois, to a small town in Arkansas called Hope. His wife, Virginia, was there. Blythe was planning to take her back to Chicago, where he was working a new job and had bought a new home for what was soon to be his new family.

Then disaster struck. The car's tire blew, sending his car veering off Highway 61 and throwing him facedown into a ditch. Blythe was only bruised, but he was knocked

▲ *This small house in Hope, Arkansas, was Bill Clinton's first home. He lived there from his birth in 1946 until his mother married her second husband when Billy was four years old.*

unconscious, and his face was buried in a few inches of water. Within hours, he was found dead.

Virginia Blythe was six months pregnant when her husband drowned. Three months later, on August 19, 1946, she gave birth to their son, William Jefferson Blythe III, who she nicknamed Billy. Virginia and Billy lived with her parents, Edith and Eldridge Cassidy, in a two-story house that had no indoor bathroom. Around the time her son turned one year old, Virginia realized that she would need to get a decent job to be able to support him. She moved to New Orleans, Louisiana, where she spent two years in nursing school.

Billy, meanwhile, lived with his "Mammaw" and "Pappaw," as he called his grandparents. They read books to him, and soon Billy was reading to them. Edith pinned playing cards to the curtains so Billy could study the numbers and learn to count. When Billy entered preschool at Miss Marie Purkins' School for Little Folks, his teachers noticed that Billy finished every project.

Learning What is "In Store"

Hope was a small town of seven thousand people when Billy was born. Back then in the South, whites and blacks did not mix together much. In fact, the section of Hope where African-Americans lived was referred to as "Colored Town."

Eldridge Cassidy owned a general store on North Hazel Street, which was on the edge of Colored Town. Therefore, he had both white and black customers, and unlike many businessmen, Eldridge treated both equally. He was kind and generous, often letting people purchase items they needed on credit.

"He knew he was part of a community," Clinton said many years later.[1]

Many people, including the future president himself, feel that Cassidy's example taught Billy to treat all people with equal compassion and caring.

Moving to Hot Springs

When Billy was around four years old, Virginia met a Buick car dealer named Roger Clinton at her father's store. The two were quickly attracted to each other and were married within months. Soon, Billy Blythe became known as "Billy Clinton."

By early 1953, when Billy was in second grade, Roger wanted a change. He sold his Buick dealership and moved Virginia and Billy to another Arkansas town called Hot

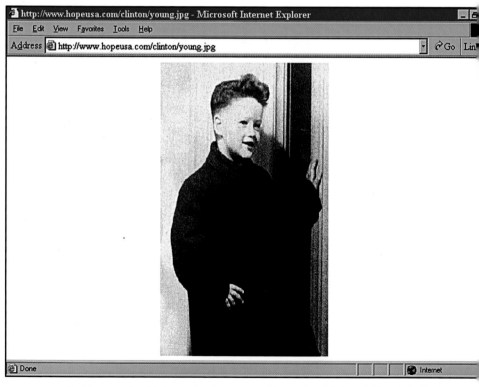

Young Billy Clinton was always considered by childhood friends to be very intelligent and mature for his age.

Springs. Full of partying and illegal gambling, Hot Springs attracted large crowds of people and had a busy nightlife that Roger and Virginia enjoyed.

Billy, meanwhile, attended a Catholic school called St. John's for the rest of second grade and all of third grade. He was enrolled in a public school, Ramble Elementary, for fourth grade. He was popular among his classmates, though sometimes his teachers had to remind Billy not to answer every question in class so quickly. That way, they told him, the other kids could participate, too. Billy enjoyed many of the same things as other kids— touch football, Monopoly, and the music of Elvis Presley.

Billy's early political interests started blossoming around this time. Virginia and Roger purchased their first black-and-white television in 1955, which was just in time for Billy to watch the Democratic National Convention in 1956.

▷ Protecting His Family

In 1956, when Billy was ten, his mother and stepfather had a son, Roger Clinton, Jr. As Roger grew, Billy played a large part in taking care of him. He often got him dressed, took him to school, and watched out for him. "I was the father," he said.[2]

As Billy grew both physically and mentally, he began taking charge more at home. Roger, Sr., had been married once before, and though Virginia did not know it when she met him, he had a history of spousal abuse. That did not change with his new family. Roger had a gambling and drinking problem, and when he lost control of his emotions, he would sometimes hit his wife or son. He was so out of control that one time, Roger even fired a bullet into the floor of the house.[3]

By the time Bill turned fourteen, he was determined to end the abuse. One day, after hearing a fight through his mother's bedroom door, Bill broke inside and ordered Roger to stop. "Hear me," said Bill, who was already six feet tall. "Never . . . ever . . . touch my mother again!"[4]

Eventually, Virginia decided to leave Roger. They divorced in May 1962, but after Roger begged Virginia to give him another chance, the couple remarried three months later. That is when Bill decided to legally change his last name to "Clinton." He hoped that by having the same last name as his mother, brother, and stepfather, the family would become closer.

Excelling in High School

Bill's high-school years were full of awards and achievements. As a tenor saxophone player, he won first prize in a statewide music competition and also formed a jazz trio, called "Three Blind Mice," with his friends Randy Goodrum and Joe Newman.

Bill remained interested in service, and joined a youth civic organization called DeMolay. People often requested that Bill run their fund-raising events for charity. In fact, the requests numbered so high that his high school principal cut them off. Bill was president of his junior class. He wanted to run for the same office during his senior year, but his principal would not let him do that either. Instead, Bill ran for class secretary—a position that would demand less time—but lost to his good friend, Carolyn Staley.

Bill's best memory of high school came in the summer of 1963, just before his senior year. He was picked as one of Arkansas' representatives to a national youth leadership conference called Boys Nation, in Washington, D.C. On a

Bill's love for the saxophone lasted way after high school. Here, President Clinton performs at his inaugural ball on January 20, 1993.

trip to the White House, Bill shook the hand of President John F. Kennedy in the Rose Garden. Four months later, Bill was sitting in class when the teacher announced that the president had been assassinated.

"He was motionless," Bill's classmate, Phil Jamison, said of his friend. "Not even a twitch on his face. Yet you could feel the anger building up inside of him."[5]

Bill was devastated, but even more determined to fulfill the goal he had set after meeting his hero: He wanted to become president.

Chapter 3 ▶

To the Top of the State, 1964–1992

When Bill Clinton graduated from high school on May 29, 1964, he was ranked fourth in his class of 363 students. Inspired by his meeting with President Kennedy and moved by Martin Luther King, Jr.'s, "I Have a Dream" speech, he felt ready to go out into the world and make a difference.

▶ Back to the Capital

Clinton chose to attend college at Georgetown University in Washington, D.C. He worked toward a degree in international affairs and also kept his hand in politics. In his

▲ During his freshman and sophomore years at Georgetown University, Clinton was elected class president. Here he is shown (far left) in his freshman year with the other class officials-(left to right) Judith Baiocchi, secretary; David Kammer, vice president; and Paul Maloy, treasurer.

freshman and sophomore years, Clinton was elected class president. During his junior year, Clinton did not run for anything. He took a job working long hours as a clerk in the office of Senator William Fulbright, whom he had met through Boys Nation. One of his main roles was the unpleasant task of compiling the names of Arkansans wounded or killed in the Vietnam War. Clinton opposed the war, and when he became involved in national politics two decades later, he would be accused of avoiding the draft.

As a senior at Georgetown, Clinton ran for president of the student body, but lost. However, there were worse disappointments. In November 1967, Clinton's stepfather died of cancer. Bill had made several trips back to Arkansas to be with Roger. Even though the two had not gotten along since Bill had confronted him years earlier, they were able to settle their differences before Roger died.

Another loss that struck Clinton deeply was the assassination of Martin Luther King, Jr., on April 4, 1968. Riots broke out over King's killing in cities across the United States, including Washington, D.C. Clinton worked as a Red Cross volunteer during those riots. First Kennedy, now King. Two of Clinton's public heroes were dead.

▷ On to Oxford

Clinton, though, kept moving forward toward a career in politics. At the urging of Senator Fulbright, he applied for (and eventually received) a Rhodes Scholarship. Awarded to only the most talented and promising students, the Rhodes Scholarship allowed Clinton to travel to England and study for up to three years at Oxford University, all expenses paid.

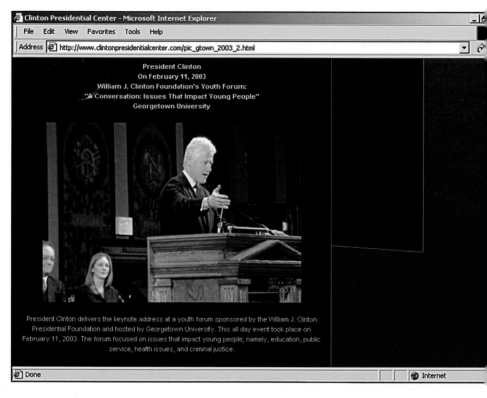

President Clinton
On February 11, 2003
William J. Clinton Foundation's Youth Forum:
"A Conversation: Issues That Impact Young People"
Georgetown University

President Clinton delivers the keynote address at a youth forum sponsored by the William J. Clinton Presidential Foundation and hosted by Georgetown University. This all day event took place on February 11, 2003. The forum focused on issues that impact young people; namely, education, public service, health issues, and criminal justice.

▲ On February 11, 2003 Bill Clinton returned to his alma mater, Georgetown University. He gave a speech sponsored by his William J. Clinton Foundation.

Clinton's main areas of study at Oxford were economics and politics. Although, he also made time to sit in on other classes and travel all around Europe. He read nearly three hundred books at Oxford during his two-year stay.

With one year left on his scholarship, Clinton chose to return to the states in the fall of 1971 to attend Yale Law School. It would be his last step before venturing into a career in politics.

At Yale, Clinton excelled at his class work and held several jobs to pay his tuition. In the library one day, he met a young woman from Chicago named Hillary

Rodham. "Look," she said to him. "If you're going to keep staring at me and I'm going to keep staring back, we should at least introduce ourselves. I'm Hillary Rodham."[1]

The pair clicked right away and began dating. They learned that they shared similar political views and both aspired to get involved in government service.

Back to Arkansas

After graduating from Yale with law degrees in 1972, Hillary took a job in Washington, D.C., while Bill, eager to begin his political career, chose to return home to Arkansas. He took a job teaching law at the University of Arkansas but quickly jumped into a campaign, running for the U.S. House of Representatives in 1974.

Throughout his years at Georgetown, Oxford, and Yale, Clinton had built a set of index cards listing all the people he had met, including important details about them. He used that network of friends to build support for his campaign. Though he lost narrowly, the exposure and experience helped him get elected as Arkansas' attorney general two years later.

A skilled organizer, Hillary Rodham had moved to Arkansas to help with Clinton's congressional campaign. They married in 1975, and she helped her husband get elected as attorney general while they both worked on Jimmy Carter's 1976 presidential campaign.

As attorney general (1977–78), Clinton viewed himself as a fighter for fairness on behalf of Arkansas' citizens. He kept a careful watch on businesses and utility companies, making sure they ran their operations fairly. If they did not, Attorney General Clinton would find out what laws they were breaking and prosecute them in court.

▷ Grabbing the Governorship

In 1978, Clinton got the opportunity he had always wanted: Governor David Pryor was not running for reelection, which meant the office was completely open. Promising to reform health care and education, Clinton easily won the governorship. He was only thirty-two at the time—the youngest governor in America.

During his first two-year term, Clinton revamped Arkansas' school system. He increased both job security and the expectations placed upon teachers, and set state tests in place for all students. Hillary set up a health-care system for people in rural Arkansas who otherwise did not have easy access to treatment.

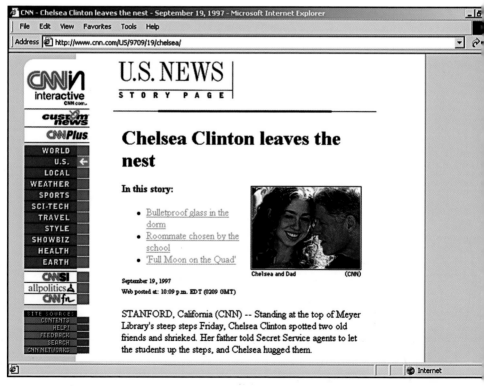

CNN - Chelsea Clinton leaves the nest - September 19, 1997 - Microsoft Internet Explorer

File　Edit　View　Favorites　Tools　Help

Address http://www.cnn.com/US/9709/19/chelsea/

U.S. NEWS | STORY PAGE

Chelsea Clinton leaves the nest

In this story:

- Bulletproof glass in the dorm
- Roommate chosen by the school
- 'Full Moon on the Quad'

Chelsea and Dad　　　(CNN)

September 19, 1997
Web posted at: 10:09 p.m. EDT (0209 GMT)

STANFORD, California (CNN) -- Standing at the top of Meyer Library's steep steps Friday, Chelsea Clinton spotted two old friends and shrieked. Her father told Secret Service agents to let the students up the steps, and Chelsea hugged them.

▲ *Chelsea Clinton is Bill and Hillary Clinton's only child. Born in 1980, she left for college while the Clintons were in the White House.*

To pay for these programs, however, higher taxes were levied on the citizens. People did not like that, and they also became angry in 1979, when thousands of Cuban refugees filled the Arkansas countryside. At President Carter's request, the refugees were supposed to stay at a military base, Fort Chaffee. There was not enough room, however, and the public-relations disaster combined with higher taxes led to Clinton's reelection defeat in 1980.

▶ Getting it Back

Though Clinton was depressed over losing his job, not all was bad. Bill and Hillary's first and only child, Chelsea, was born that same year. Now a family man, the youngest ex-governor in America worked on getting his job back. While the new governor, Frank White, broke apart many Clinton programs, the ex-governor quietly prepared to run again. He traveled from town to town, and asked people what he did wrong and what he could do better next time.

"And they would tell me—in great, stunning, brutal detail," he said. "They then gave me a second chance to serve."[2]

In 1982, Clinton won the job back. Over the next ten years, he continued to revamp education in Arkansas and also gained national recognition. Clinton was elected to four more terms before launching a full-scale campaign for the presidential election of 1992.

After winning the Democratic nomination, Clinton faced incumbent President George Herbert Walker Bush, a Republican, and billionaire Ross Perot, an independent. During the campaign, particularly in the midst of debates, Clinton's smooth, easy way of speaking made him appear far more comfortable than Bush or Perot. Plus, the

▲ *Governor Clinton faces President George H. W. Bush in a presidential debate on October 19, 1992, at Michigan State University.*

nation's economy was faltering, and people blamed President Bush.

Clinton and his running mate, Senator Al Gore from Tennessee, won the general election in November 1992 with 43 percent of the popular vote. Bush had received 37 percent, and Perot attained 19 percent.

At the relatively young age of forty-five, Bill Clinton had achieved his lifelong dream: He was going to be president of the United States.

A Washington Welcome, 1993–1996

When William Jefferson Clinton became the forty-second president of the United States on January 20, 1993, he promised to turn around the stumbling economy.

"To renew America, we must be bold," Clinton proclaimed in his inaugural address. "We must do what no generation has had to do before. We must invest more in

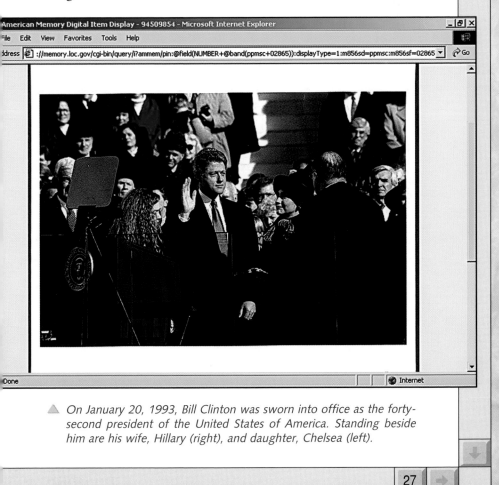

American Memory Digital Item Display - 94509854 - Microsoft Internet Explorer

File   Edit   View   Favorites   Tools   Help

Address ://memory.loc.gov/cgi-bin/query/l?ammem/pin:@field(NUMBER+@band(ppmsc+02865)):displayType=1:m856sd=ppmsc:m856sf=02865   Go

Done   Internet

▲ On January 20, 1993, Bill Clinton was sworn into office as the forty-second president of the United States of America. Standing beside him are his wife, Hillary (right), and daughter, Chelsea (left).

our own people, in their jobs, in their future, and at the same time cut our massive debt. And we must do so in a world in which we must compete for every opportunity."[1]

▶ Big Ideas

The first Democrat in the White House since Jimmy Carter left in 1981, Clinton came to Washington with big promises. Fixing the economy was one. Placing women in higher positions of power was another. Perhaps the most powerful woman in the country was Hillary Clinton. The traditional role of a first lady is to serve as the social host at the White House and speak out on a few select, but usually nonpolitical issues. For example, Barbara Bush had pushed literacy. Before her, Nancy Reagan promoted an antidrug program.

Hillary Clinton was different. She took an active role in policy making, much like Eleanor Roosevelt had done alongside her husband, Franklin, in the 1930s and 1940s. She consulted with the president and his staff on nearly every major decision, and played a leading role on some issues. That made some people uneasy, but she did not apologize for it.

"I suppose I could have stayed home and baked cookies and had teas," she said during the 1992 campaign, "but what I decided to do was to fulfill my profession which I entered before my husband was in public life."[2]

Mrs. Clinton wrote three books during her time in the White House, including one on parenting called *It Takes a Village to Raise a Child*. President and Mrs. Clinton prided themselves on being good parents to their daughter, Chelsea, who was twelve when the family moved into the White House. They did everything possible to keep Chelsea out of the public eye. She was never allowed to

▲ *Hillary Rodham Clinton broke the mold of the usual first lady. Unlike some of her predecessors, Hillary took an active role in her husband's administration, including being responsible for instituting a national health care plan.*

give interviews, and staff members were forbidden to discuss her with reporters.

Chelsea was a good student who loved to read, both by herself and with her parents. She had a cat, Socks, who she brought with her to the White House from Arkansas. Later in his presidency, Clinton added a dog, named Buddy, to the family.

▷ Losing Health Care

One of President Clinton's grandest plans was to institute a national health care plan that would guarantee that any American would be able to receive medical treatment when needed.

Turning his health care plan from an idea into an actual law would take a lot of work. Soon after the inauguration, that job was assigned to Mrs. Clinton. Working with a team of advisers, she put together a complicated proposal that was over 1,300 pages long.

Wherever the president or first lady traveled, they tried to gather support for the health care bill. The team that helped develop the bill worked hard to get Congress to support it. Republicans, though, had their own ideas for health care reform, and the big insurance companies fought against Clinton's idea, fearing it would hurt their businesses.

In the end, the health care bill could not pass through Congress. With so many complex rules and money issues involved, the bill never had a real chance of becoming law. Though the first lady was heavily criticized for the failure, the president said the blame belonged to him. "She was operating within constraints that we now know are impossible," the president said a few years later. "But it was my mistake, not hers. All she did was what she was asked to do."[3]

Early Successes

Clinton did have some success in his first two years. He wanted to reduce the deficit (the amount of money the United States government was overspending) in the federal budget and submitted a plan to Congress. It narrowly passed in the House and received a fifty-fifty vote in the Senate. Vice President Gore cast the tie-breaking vote, and the bill was passed.

"The president was relieved," said Secretary of Labor Robert Reich. "Had he lost, he would not just have lost the budget battle, he would have lost enormous political face. The message would have been, 'This guy cannot deliver.'"[4]

▲ *Al Gore served as vice president under Bill Clinton throughout the president's time in the White House.*

Clinton's ideas for opening up business exchanges with other countries became law in November 1993 when the North American Free Trade Agreement (NAFTA) gave the United States, Canada, and Mexico a free trade zone.

In August 1994, Clinton signed a bill that would channel $30 billion into preventing crime. Also passed was the "Brady Bill," a gun-control law named after James Brady. He had been President Ronald Reagan's press secretary. Brady was injured when someone attempted to assassinate Reagan in 1981.

Dealing with foreign leaders and problems in other countries was new for Clinton. He was successful, though, in helping to restore peace to a war-torn part of the globe. In the early 1990s, a bitter war was being waged in Bosnia, a country in Eastern Europe, between Serbs, Croats, and

Muslims. Clinton brought members of the groups to Dayton, Ohio, and spent three weeks working out a peace agreement. He also sent twenty thousand United States troops to Bosnia as peacekeepers.

▷ Losing the House

After spending twelve years working with presidents (Ronald Reagan and George H. W. Bush) from their own party, the Republicans were eager to seize control of Congress. A group of them worked out a series of promises called the "Contract with America."

It worked. In the fall of 1994, Republicans took back control of the House of Representatives and the Senate. It was the first time since 1954 that the Republicans won

▲ Republican House Speaker Newt Gingrich (left) constantly clashed with Democratic President Clinton (right).

control of both branches. Newt Gingrich, a loud and outspoken critic of Clinton, became Speaker of the House of Representatives.

Clinton and Gingrich would engage in many political battles over the next few years. The biggest came near the end of 1995. The Republican leadership had written and passed a bill that would balance the budget—as Clinton wanted to do—and cut taxes. The problem, in Clinton's eyes was, that the bill also included deep cuts to health care and education.

Clinton vetoed the bill and offered to work out a deal with the Republicans. The Republicans refused. Over the next several weeks, the White House and Congress fell into gridlock—meaning no progress was made towards a compromise. Meanwhile, the government was running out of money. In November, the federal government actually shut down because it was unable to pay most of its employees for coming to work.

While eight hundred thousand workers stayed home, Clinton and the Republicans made some progress. Six days later, the government reopened, but not for long. In the middle of December, workers were sent home again—this time, for three weeks.

Republicans believed that the government shutdown would pressure President Clinton into giving in to their demands. The effect, though, was opposite: Polls showed that voters blamed the Republicans for the shutdown, and the situation actually helped boost Clinton's popularity.

Big Wins and Blunders, 1996–2001

Heading into the 1996 election, the Clinton-Gore team was facing a huge historical challenge: No Democratic president had been elected to a second term since Franklin D. Roosevelt. In addition, Clinton and the people who worked for him always seemed to be under investigation for suspected wrongdoings. Investigators looked into the administration's use of classified FBI files, firings in the White House's travel office, and methods use to raise funds for the 1996 presidential campaign.

The only investigation that led to major trouble for the president at the time was called the "Whitewater affair." It centered on alleged wrongdoings by then Governor and

Mrs. Clinton in an Arkansas land deal during the 1980s. The Whitewater investigation stretched far beyond the land deal and into other areas of Clinton's life, both present and past. The findings would lead to his impeachment.

◀ *The Whitewater affair and its investigation would plague Bill Clinton's second term in office. The president addressed the issue of his wife's involvement at this January 1996 press conference.*

First-Term Accomplishments

As his first term neared its end, Clinton's list of accomplishments had grown significantly from his rocky first months in office. Along with the crime bill and trade agreements, he had cut the deficit in half. He had signed a bill that reformed welfare (the financial assistance program for poor people) by giving power back to each individual state. Clinton had also signed the Family and Medical Leave Act, which guaranteed that people could take time off from work to care for young children or a sick family member.

Beyond that, Clinton proved that he could be effective in foreign relations. He pushed the island country of Haiti to recognize its elected president instead of a military dictator. He eased nuclear tensions with North Korea and ordered bombing strikes against Iraq when the Middle Eastern country violated the terms of the post-Persian Gulf War peace agreement.

Winning Again

In the 1996 election, the Clinton-Gore team was facing Republican nominee Robert Dole, a former senator, and his running mate, ex-Congressman Jack Kemp. Independent Ross Perot also ran again, but the three-way race was not even close. Clinton captured over 45 million votes, while Dole received just under 38 million. Perot's total was close to 8 million—less than half the votes he earned in 1992.

"The greatest progress we have made, and the greatest progress we have yet to make, is the human heart," Clinton said in his second inaugural address on January 20, 1997. "In the end, all the world's wealth and a thousand armies

are no match for the strength and decency of the human spirit."[1]

Much of Clinton's work during his second term followed that theme of humanity. In places like Northern Ireland and Israel, where bloody battles had been going on for decades, Clinton used his influence as leader of the world's most powerful country to push for peace. He worked hard to help America's former nemesis, Russia, reestablish a strong government after it had undergone deep changes in the late 1980s. He also kept a watchful eye on Iraqi leader Saddam Hussein, who was suspected of building weapons of mass destruction. When Hussein repeatedly refused to cooperate with weapons-inspection

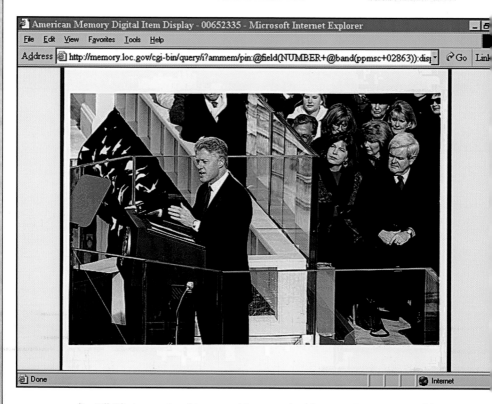

▲ Bill Clinton makes his second inaugural address on January 20, 1997.

teams from the United Nations, Clinton and British Prime Minister Tony Blair ordered air strikes.

Within the country, Clinton continued to work with a Republican-controlled Congress. His major areas of focus were education, the environment, and health care. He concentrated on helping working people by successfully pushing for an increase in the minimum wage and promoting programs that encouraged people to work. Under Clinton, national unemployment numbers were the lowest in thirty years.

As the Internet boomed, computer technology companies (called "dot-coms") grew at an amazing pace in the 1990s. Congress cut taxes in 1997, and the federal budget had a $70 billion surplus (extra money) in 1998. People were working, and their investments were doing well. Under Clinton's watch, the economy was strong.

An Impeachable Offense

In January 1994, Attorney General Janet Reno had followed the president's orders to appoint an independent counsel to look into the Clintons' role in the Whitewater land deal. The president's thinking was that by appointing an independent counsel, a person who could investigate without any fear of interference, the facts would be made clear that he and his wife had done nothing wrong.

At the time, the law granted an independent counsel the power to hire a large staff and take an investigation in any direction that he or she wanted. In other words, if the independent counsel happened to learn of something else the president may have done wrong, that could be investigated, too.

That became a huge problem for Clinton.

In January 1998, *Newsweek* magazine reported that the president had participated in an inappropriate, intimate relationship with a young woman. That was nothing new. Talk about Clinton's personal life had began long before he was even elected president. This was different, though, because the young woman, Monica Lewinsky, had been a White House intern. The alleged relationship had occurred in the Oval Office.

Clinton strongly denied it, but Independent Counsel Kenneth Starr was investigating the situation. By summer, it was learned that Clinton had indeed participated in the relationship. Many felt he had lied about it while testifying under oath.

Lying under oath is called *perjury*. It is against the law for anyone, but for the president, the consequences are even worse. On December 19, 1998, the House of Representatives voted to impeach Clinton for perjury and obstruction of justice.

Impeachment is when the House of Representatives votes to bring the president to trial before the Senate. If the president is convicted, he will be removed from office. Prior to Clinton, only one president, Andrew Johnson, had been impeached, back in 1868. Johnson was not removed.

The trial began on January 7, 1999. It was run by William Rehnquist, Chief Justice of the Supreme Court, and lasted one month. A group of Republican congressmen presented the case against Clinton to the one hundred members of the Senate, who voted on each of the two charges.

Neither charge received the sixty-seven votes that were needed to convict and remove the president. On February 12, 1999, he was cleared of impeachment charges. Bill Clinton's job was safe, and he could move ahead.

"I want to say again to the American people how sorry I am for what I said and did to trigger these events," Clinton said. "This can be and this must be a time of reconciliation and renewal for America."[2]

▲ In the second presidential impeachment trial ever to occur in United States history, the Senate acquitted Bill Clinton of perjury and obstruction of justice charges on Friday, February 12, 1999.

Clinton's Impact, 2001 to Present

In December 2000, one month before he was to leave office, Bill Clinton held one of his final press conferences in the White House. He was reflecting on the two terms he had spent fulfilling his lifelong dream—becoming president of the United States.

"I have loved these eight years," he said. "You know, I read in the history books how other presidents say the

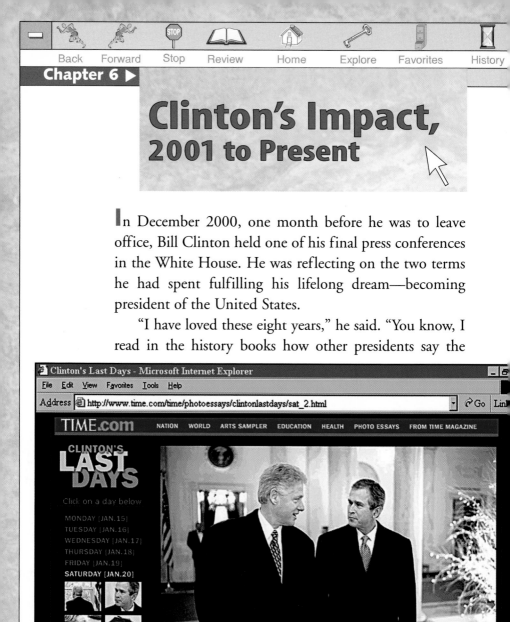

Clinton's Last Days - Microsoft Internet Explorer

File Edit View Favorites Tools Help

Address http://www.time.com/time/photoessays/clintonlastdays/sat_2.html   ⟋Go Lin

TIME.com   NATION WORLD ARTS SAMPLER EDUCATION HEALTH PHOTO ESSAYS FROM TIME MAGAZINE

CLINTON'S
LAST
DAYS

Click on a day below

MONDAY [JAN.15]
TUESDAY [JAN.16]
WEDNESDAY [JAN.17]
THURSDAY [JAN.18]
FRIDAY [JAN.19]
SATURDAY [JAN.20]

◀ previous   next ▶

Clinton gives President Bush the lay of the land. "Bush really connects," the outgoing president later told friends. "It's a mistake to underestimate him."

Internet

▲ The United States president is only allowed to serve two terms. After having done so, Bill Clinton was succeeded by Republican George W. Bush in 2001.

White House is like a penitentiary, and every motive they have is suspect. Even George Washington complained he was treated as a common thief. And they all say they cannot wait to get away." Clinton looked at the reporters and added, "I don't know what the heck they're talking about."[1]

Everyone laughed. They knew the president was joking. Even after he survived impeachment, Clinton's last two years in the White House were spent dealing with investigations and squabbling with the Republican-led Congress. Though the impeachment proceedings ended in early 1999, the various investigations that went with it did not wrap up until shortly after Clinton left Washington in 2001.

Clinton and Congress argued over tax cuts and health-care issues during his final months in office. They did agree to grant China "normal trade" status, which meant United States and Chinese companies could freely build relationships and exchange goods.

Since United States law limits presidents to two elected terms of four years each, Clinton could not run again in 2000. He did, however, keep a close watch on two campaigns that fall. Hillary Clinton was running for a Senate seat in New York, and Vice President Al Gore was campaigning for the presidency. Mrs. Clinton won, while Vice President Gore lost a close election to George W. Bush, the son of the former president.

The Clinton Legacy

Despite the controversies that swirled around him, Clinton left office as an enormously popular president. His approval rating during his final full month in the White House was 66 percent, one of the highest ever for a president in his second term.

Why was Clinton so popular? Most historians give a simple answer: The economy was strong. Presidents who oversee a nation with a strong economy, such as Clinton and Ronald Reagan, get high ratings from everyday people. Presidents during a time of high unemployment, rising prices or a struggling stock market typically do not even get a second term. Jimmy Carter and George H. W. Bush are examples of that.

"I believe people send presidents to do certain jobs, particularly when there are certain, important, pressing needs," said Skip Rutherford, a friend of Clinton for thirty years. "When Bill Clinton went to Washington in

▲ *After leaving the White House on January 20, 2001, the Clintons left for New York, where Hillary had been elected to the U.S. Senate. Although Bill Clinton is now a private citizen, he is expected to still have an influence in the nation's politics.*

1993, he had one major objective and that was to turn the economy around, and he delivered."[2]

New Homes, New Activities

As they prepared to leave the White House, the Clintons bought two homes: one just outside New York City, and the other in Washington, D.C. That would allow President Clinton to set up his office in New York City, and give Senator Clinton homes both in her state and in the capital. Chelsea, meanwhile, was finishing college at Stanford University in California. She later studied at Oxford, just like her father.

Clinton also decided to build his presidential library in the Arkansas capital of Little Rock. Former presidents in modern history often have a library that houses the millions of documents associated with their administration.

Clinton was fifty-four years old when he left office, a decade or two younger than most ex-presidents. Jimmy Carter was fifty-six when he left the White House in 1981. Carter set up an organization called the Carter Center, which he uses to promote health and peace around the globe. Wanting to do something similar, Clinton set up the William J. Clinton Foundation, which he hopes will help him continue to make a difference in areas such as education, health care, human rights, and world peace.

Unlike Carter, Clinton left the White House owing millions of dollars in legal fees. To help pay those, he signed a multimillion-dollar book deal and began giving speeches around the world, charging between $100,000 and $200,000 per talk.

"After I get my legal bills paid and my houses paid and all that kind of stuff," he said, "I'd like to get to where I can just spend a hundred percent of my time on public service."[3]

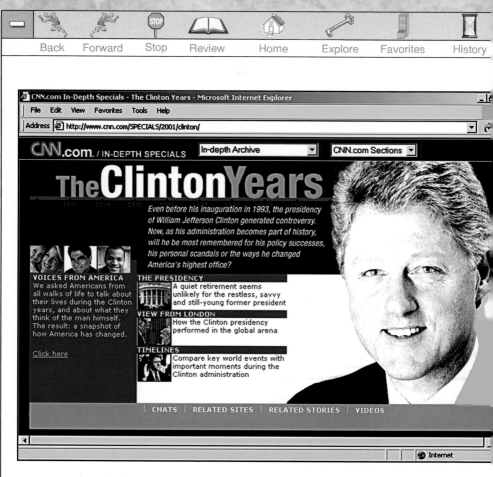

CNN.com In-Depth Specials - The Clinton Years - Microsoft Internet Explorer

File   Edit   View   Favorites   Tools   Help

Address http://www.cnn.com/SPECIALS/2001/clinton/

CNN.com / IN-DEPTH SPECIALS   In-depth Archive   CNN.com Sections

The ClintonYears

Even before his inauguration in 1993, the presidency of William Jefferson Clinton generated controversy. Now, as his administration becomes part of history, will he be most remembered for his policy successes, his personal scandals or the ways he changed America's highest office?

VOICES FROM AMERICA
We asked Americans from all walks of life to talk about their lives during the Clinton years, and about what they think of the man himself. The result: a snapshot of how America has changed.

Click here

THE PRESIDENCY
A quiet retirement seems unlikely for the restless, savvy and still-young former president

VIEW FROM LONDON
How the Clinton presidency performed in the global arena

TIMELINES
Compare key world events with important moments during the Clinton administration

CHATS   RELATED SITES   RELATED STORIES   VIDEOS

Internet

Bill Clinton's presidency will be remembered as a success for lowering the poverty rate and creating a strong economy. He will also be known for the ongoing heath care crisis and the scandals he was a part of.

How Clinton will be remembered by future generations is still to be determined—it is likely that he has a long life of service ahead of him. Some people even believe he will run for office again, perhaps as a mayor or senator.

Whatever he chooses to do, this much is certain: Bill Clinton will be remembered as a president who, either despite of, or because of all his faults, had an unforgettable impact on American history.

Chapter 1. Hope for America, July 16, 1992

1. Bonnie Angelo, *First Mothers: The Women Who Shaped the Presidents* (New York: William Morrow, 2000), p. 393.

2. Ibid.

3. Dan Balz, "Clinton vows to 'change America;' In accepting party's nomination Democrat assails 'forces of greed.'" *Washington Post,* July 17, 1992, p. A1.

4. Ibid.

Chapter 2. Small Town Boy, Big Dreams, 1946–1964

1. Philip B. Kunhardt, Jr., Philip B. Kunhardt III, and Peter W. Kunhardt, *The American President* (New York: Riverhead Books, 1999), p. 432.

2. David Rubel, *Mr. President: The Human Side of America's Chief Executives* (Alexandria, Va.: Time-Life Books, 1998), p. 250.

3. William A. DeGregorio, *The Complete Book of U.S. Presidents: From George Washington to Bill Clinton* (New York, Wings Books, 1997), p. 704.

4. Bonnie Angelo, *First Mothers: The Women Who Shaped the Presidents* (New York: William Morrow, 2000), p. 379.

5. David Maraniss, *First in His Class* (New York: Simon & Schuster, 1995), p. 44.

Chapter 3. To the Top of the State, 1964–1992

1. David Maraniss, *First in His Class* (New York: Simon & Schuster, 1995), p. 247.

2. Philip B. Kunhardt, Jr., Philip B. Kunhardt III, and Peter W. Kunhardt, *The American President* (New York: Riverhead Books, 1999), p. 432.

Chapter 4. A Washington Welcome, 1993–1996

1. Bill Clinton, "First Inaugural Address (January 21, 1993)," *Inaugural Addresses of the Presidents,* n.d., <http://www.bartleby.com/124/pres64.html> (May 16, 2003).

2. *Nightline* Transcripts, "Making Hillary Clinton an Issue," *Frontline*, March 26, 1992, <http://www.pbs.org/wgbh/pages/frontline/shows/clinton/etc/03261992.html> (May 16, 2003).

3. Joe Klein, *The Natural: The Misunderstood Presidency of Bill Clinton* (New York: Doubleday, 2002), pp. 126–127.

4. ABC News Internet Ventures, "The Clinton Years–Promise and Defeat," *Nightline Frontline*, 2000, <http://www.pbs.org/wgbh/pages/frontline/shows/clinton/chapters/3.html> (May 16, 2003).

Chapter 5. Big Wins and Blunders, 1996–2001

1. Bill Clinton, "Second Inaugural Address (January 20, 1997)," *Inaugural Addresses of the Presidents*, n.d., <http://www.bartleby.com/124/pres65.html> (May 16, 2003).

2. Bob Woodward, *Shadow* (New York: Simon & Schuster, 1999), p. 513.

Chapter 6. Clinton's Impact, 2001 to Present

1. Randy Lilleston, "We probably haven't seen the last of Clinton," *CNN.com*, 2001, <http://www.cnn.com/SPECIALS/2001/clinton/presidency/presidency.html> (May 16, 2003).

2. Ibid.

3. James Fallows, "Post President for Life," *The Atlantic Monthly*, March 2003, p. 64.

Further Reading

Cohen, Daniel. *The Impeachment of William Jefferson Clinton.* Brookfield, Conn.: Twenty-first Century Books, 2000.

Feinstein, Stephen. *The 1990s: From the Persian Gulf War to Y2K.* Berkeley Heights, N.J.: Enslow Publishers, Inc., 2001.

Gaines, Ann Graham. *William Jefferson Clinton: Our Forty-Second President.* Chanhassen, Minn.: The Child's World, 2001.

Gullo, James. *Hillary Rodham Clinton.* Farmington Hills, Mich.: Gale Group, 2004.

Heinrichs, Ann. *William Jefferson Clinton.* Minneapolis, Minn.: Compass Point Books, 2002.

Howard, Todd, ed. *William J. Clinton.* San Diego, Calif.: Greenhaven Press, Inc., 2000.

Kjelle, Marylou Morano. *Arkansas: A MyReportLinks.com Book.* Berkeley Heights, N.J.: MyReportLinks.com Books, 2003.

Lucas, Eileen. *Al Gore: Vice President.* Brookfield, Conn.: Millbrook Press, Inc., 1999.

Marcovitz, Hal. *Bill Clinton.* Broomall, Pa.: Mason Crest Publishers, 2003.

Schuman, Michael A. *Bill Clinton, Revised Edition.* Berkeley Heights, N.J.: Enslow Publishers, Inc., 2003.

Index